QUOTES FROM THE QUIVER

Dante P. Galiber, MD, FACC

AuthorHouse™
1663 Liberty Drive
Bloomington, IN 47403
www.authorhouse.com
Phone: 1 (800) 839-8640

Because of the dynamic nature of the Internet, any web addresses or links contained in this book may have changed
since publication and may no longer be valid. The views expressed in this work are solely those of the author and do not
necessarily reflect the views of the publisher, and the publisher hereby disclaims any responsibility for them.

Any people depicted in stock imagery provided by Getty Images are models,
and such images are being used for illustrative purposes only.
Certain stock imagery © Getty Images.

This book is printed on acid-free paper.

ISBN: 978-1-7283-1124-1 (hc)
ISBN: 978-1-5462-2702-1 (sc)
ISBN: 978-1-5462-2701-4 (e)

Library of Congress Control Number: 2018901313

Print information available on the last page.

Published by AuthorHouse 01/14/2020

Contents

Dedicated to:

Wife and Daughter: Yvonne Ashley and Dominique Ashley
Parents: Andre Anthony Galiber, SR, MD, FACR* and Edith Rose Lewis Galiber, RN*
Sister: Lisa Marie Galiber*
Brothers and sisters
Father-in-law and Mother-in-law: Fred Ashley, SR* and Elsie Ashley*
Family and friends

*In memoriam

Dearest Yvonne Ashley,

"Fret for your father not, for he has gone nowhere except in your heart!"

Yours,

Dante Pierre

Acknowledgments

Editor: Lynn Suruma
Graphic Artist: Chelsea Galiber
Graphic Arts Consultant: Djeneé T. Dunn
Artistic Consultant: Gerville R. Larsen
Photographer: Alda E. Anduze

PREFACE

Wise words from the voices of the known or unknown should never fall on deaf ears.

Many of the quotations in *Quotes from the Quiver* (QFTQ) were inspired by a pentad of thematic creativity: *Time, History, Evolution, Medicine, and Environment (THEME)*. "Inspiration, dedication, and persistence are a wordsmith's trilogy of creativity." These attributes are the driving force that puts one's deep thoughts on display for others to ponder.

Interactions with people and deep inquiry fueled these words of wisdom, which were often powered by alliteration, such as "War is better understood through the opaque mettle of passions, principles, and politics than through the polished metal of bullets, bombs, and bayonets." *QFTQ* also covers a variety of topics that are not limited to *THEME*. They are categorized into specific chapters for ease of use and remembrance. Some of these other topics include *Life and Death, Racism,* and *Past, Present, and Future.*

Time, an abstract concept, is the "master note taker" of all things, living and nonliving. In our universe, we are in a time continuum that is well beyond the scope and theme of this book. Quotes serve at least three purposes: minimizing time, word usage, and the distance one needs to travel to attain wisdom and understanding. With some "time" on my hands I contributed some pithy quotes to the world's long list of notable ones about *Time*: "The best prophet is time," "Time is always a good predictor of what will happen," and "Being an enemy of time is truly a waste of time" are some of *QFTQ's* quotable time quotes.

History tells the story of where we have come from, whether it is recorded or not. The world as it stands is the summation of all mankind's histories. Understanding and appreciating it is paramount to peace, harmony, and purpose. "History is the thread of our existence" exemplifies this concept and leads us to accept that our history, much like our lives, is as tenuous as a thread and must be preserved by all means. "History never changes, but changes can make history" is a paradoxical but truthful statement. We have seen this concept come true with the changes in our social and moral cultural dynamics and the advent of historical revisionism to get closer to the truth of our collective existence.

Because I am a man of science, *Evolution* is a category that has fostered much thought for me. It is a mechanism that is empowered by time, engineered by genetic pressure, and exposed by the environment to attain a particular future in which not all species will be a part. The quote "Three things are true about the universe and evolution: they are in constant flux, they are real, and they couldn't care less about the whims of man" exemplifies that evolution is bound to happen whether man is a believer or a non-believer, and that this process occurs in a universe in which man is essentially a non-factor.

As a practicing cardiologist and physician, I have a captive audience with patients with whom I can talk about "Making *Medicine* Meaningful." I have had deep discussions about the doctor-patient relationship and how it should foster a trust and a bond for good living. A number of *QFTQ's* quotes have materialized from my doctor-patient relationships and among them are: "Some diseases are not discovered; they are habitually invented"; "Save more souls than the soul you have"; "Patient disease hysteria is fearing the unlikely more than the likely"; and, "A physician's patient care mission is twofold: treat disease and eliminate fear." Often, I have to allay a patient's fear of starting new medications or receiving vaccinations. Paradoxically, some patients fear the smaller risk of medical compliance more than the bigger risk of medical non-compliance. These words are offered as food for thought to gain a better understanding of how men and women charged with "healing hands" can improve the human condition.

The *Environment* is a topic involving climate change, global warming, and Mother Earth. This topic has been hotly debated in scientific and non-scientific circles. I believe that we must pay close attention to—and prevent—global warming, which will adversely affect all earthlings. The quotes, "Man is Earth's only harmful earthling," "Climate change is real and Mother Earth cannot be bargained with," and "Climate change will eliminate life's comforts" are some that exemplify the respect and appreciation that we should have for our planet and the urgency with which we should address global warming.

QFTQ is a collection of 458 quotations that were inspired by many factors in my life. An original thought as the basis of each, these quotations can be used as a direct link to success and understanding. Because "There is no good path to nowhere," we must first choose a good place and then follow any honorable path no matter how circuitous and long to get there. As with any written work it is to be hoped that the words on these pages will serve as an inspiration to others to find glimmers of logic and lifelong learning in our chaotic and cluttered world.

Dante P. Galiber, MD, FACP, FACC, FASNC
Nuclear and Noninvasive Cardiologist
Major, Virgin Islands Army National Guard

FOREWORD

Dr. Dante P. Galiber has written a collection of quotations as a gift to his community. Many of his sayings are gleaned from his long study and practice as a medical doctor, as well as from his insights as one of seven children, as a father, and as a husband.

Quotes from the Quiver is organized under relevant and easily identifiable themes, such as *Time* and *Evolution*. These headings also reveal that the book can be light and convivial, with categories such as *Friends* and *Mother Earth*, but also socially relevant and even political, with themes such as *Racism* and *Privilege*. The sections are clear and helpful for navigating the book, and for selective readers to find what they are looking for. Often, Dr. Galiber will rephrase a quote, switching around the subject and object in such a way as to offer clarity for the reader, as well as to drive his point home.

Many of the most poignant quotes seem to arise out of Dr. Galiber's own life journey — one clearly of hard work and determination. He was valedictorian of his high-school class and went on to become a successful cardiologist, and a Major in the Virgin Islands Army National Guard. His categories entitled *Achievement* and *Medicine* offer, to me, the most unique insights. These are the ones that a college student might put on a poster and hang on a dorm room wall or, perhaps, that a motivational speaker might pull from to make a speech.

Among my favorites are "Achievement is inversely related to comfort" and "Some things work better when you don't use them."

Reading *Quotes from the Quiver* allows for some laughter and some deep thinking. Dr. Galiber's readers will be grateful for it.

— Tiphanie Yanique, Professor of English and Creative Writing, most recently author of *Land of Love and Drowning, I am the Virgin Islands,* and *How to Escape from a Leper Colony.*

CHAPTERS

1. Accomplishment/Achievement

- Accomplishment occurs when dedication outweighs procrastination.

- Achievement is inversely related to comfort.

- There should be no talk of the things you have not done.

- One achieves more by leaving one's comfort zone.

- Perfection demands the inoculation of natural born talents with time and determination.

2. Beliefs, Biases, and Facts

- Because you will never believe anything I say, I choose to just listen and keep my mouth shut.

- I am not going to organize your biases into the lies that they are. Keep talking. You are doing it for me.

- FACTS are Firmly Accepted Concrete Theories, Sir.

- Fact-free believers in our fun-fact-filled universe are imprisoned by their ignorance.

- Facts, figures, and feelings make for good writing on just about anything.

- Your understanding of the facts is merely superficial. They are best verified by those with more profound introspection, intelligence, and integrity.

- There are infinitely fewer facts than fiction so just remember the facts.

- For every finite fact there is infinite fiction.

3. Direction

- Starting on your journey in the right direction is a small victory toward your destination.

- There is no good path to nowhere.

- Commitment to directionless pursuits only brings misery to the pursuer.

- There is no difference between a headstrong and a heartfelt wrong life choice.

- Pursuing your dreams will enrich your soul.

- Planning for contingencies is what good planning really is.

- With any kind of planning second best must be near best.

- An organized mind is always on the right path.

4. Environment, Mother Earth, and the Universe

- On Earth, we are a couple of blown lightbulbs away from being cavemen.

- The only harmful earthling is human.

- Humans are Earth's most ungrateful guests.

- From viruses to bacteria to invertebrates to the mighty blue whales, none does more harm to humans than humans.

- We need not make Earth our enemy, for we will lose every skirmish, extinguish any light, and vanquish any hope for survival. We need to console her when she is sad, repair her when she is hurt, and praise her for her unique hospitality in an inhospitable universe.

- Climate change will eliminate life's comforts for all earthlings.

- Climate change deniers are inherently intolerant of facts and indifferent to intelligence.

- Global warming needs more than a chilly response from climate deniers.

- We are running out of time to make peace with Mother Nature and climate change.

- Climate change is real and Mother Earth cannot be bargained with.

- Humans should let Earth decide what she wants, or they will get what she gives.

- Global warming is the tipping point at which humanity's greed has surpassed its willingness to coexist with nature as we know it.

- Those who worship money and profits over climate change will one day seek refuge from the very thing they deny, and no amount of money or prayers can be used as bargaining chips.

- If Earth had a choice, she would not choose humans as her keepers.

- The laws of the universe have never been wrong. Those of humans have seldom been right.

- Man is Earth's only harmful earthling.

5. Evolution

- Evolution, energy, and the environment are the triad of human existence.

- Evolutionary pressures have led us to the point of organizational chaos.

- Selective evolutionary procrastination is part of species design.

- Those who do not believe that humans are just on an evolutionary curve are imprisoned by ignorance of universal design.

- Three things are true about the universe and evolution: they are in constant flux, they are real, and they couldn't care less about the whims of man.

- Four billion years of evolution have created your mind, body, and soul. Brief moments of vanity can vanquish them all.

- Evolution, the universe, and our existence are there for us to study, not to refute.

- Evolutionarily, all roads led from Africa.

- Evolutionary pressures bend toward obesity because of human intervention.

- Evolutionary diversity is a mechanism for species' survival that humans have adversely tipped the balance in their favor.

- Evolution favors diversity, and so should humans.

- Evolution is nature's "this for that".

6. Friends and Relationships

- A "meaningful" friendship is redundant.

- The friendships I trust most are, often, not human.

- A perfect friend has many imperfections.

- Striving for perfection in a friendship is not what friendships are all about.

- I may not be the best friend of my best friend. Friendships are funny that way.

- Your best friend and your worst enemy have at least one thing in common: you.

- Sadly, people and politics both define and divide us.

- How can I choose my battles with you when you offer none to choose from?

- Getting an emotional response from a friend should not be like trying to unlock Fort Knox, where you get nothing of what you do want, or to open Pandora's Box, where you get everything of what you don't want.

- The bonds that join soul mates are the experiences of lifelong living and loving.

7. History

- History is the thread of our existence.

- History ends at the very moment that our present begins.

- History, like time, is bookmarked by nothingness on one end and infinity on the other.

- The future of our history is made by the actions of our present.

- History never changes, but changes can make history.

- If you do not know your own history, then you will not have the power to make it.

- Being proud of one's history does not give license to disparage another's.

- Our flesh and bones are woven into the inner fabric of the soil, sand, and substance of this country.

- Forget our history, and you lose the past; forget our children, and you lose the future.

- Telling one's history through music is a rhythmic way to remember it.

- How truthful can a history of the vanquished be when told by the voices of the victors?

- There is no one true, balanced history of the victors and the vanquished.

- Historical clarity is achieved only when the oppressed have a voice.

- Paying heed to history means repeating the good and understanding the bad.

- Fortunately, for humanity's sake, the South's demise was mired in taxation of cows and crops instead of coins and chattel.

- The American Civil War proved that a taxed cow is not worth the weight of a taxed coin.

- A history without the explicit and integral plight of the ravages of slavery is not worth telling.

- The history of any country should be told by the ones who lived its horrors.

- We are challenged to report corrected history in order to decrease the effects of racism and foster self-pride.

- Historical revisionism is the process of bringing realism to the distorted history of the victors at the behest of the vanquished.

- Revisionist history is the history of the silenced and enslaved for whom the present has given the voice that the past never did.

- Historical correctness gives equal voice and valor to the victors and the vanquished.

- History is warped by the negative influence of ethnic and religious bias.

- The curve of history is bent toward truth, knowledge, and acceptance.

8. Humanity

- By all accounts humanity's oneness is African.

- It is safe to say that all of humanity is African.

- Restoration of our humanity is central to eliminating social, political, and economic disparities.

- Propaganda links racism and sexism in perpetual conflict with human decency.

- Humanity has never been apolitical.

- With humanity imperfection is always more authentic than perfection.

- Human cultural and social expansion have always been at the expense of humanity.

- The human condition is adversely affected by the industrial globalization of agriculture.

- Humanity encourages us to learn and share experiences to reduce suffering and advance progress.

- Humanity is coordinated compassion among all the variations that humans represent.

- There is always perfect alignment with two of anything except humanity and human thought.

9. Ideas, Concepts, and Other Important Thoughts

- One's creative thinking and leadership skills are often mirrored by the character and actions of those being developed and led.

- One must learn to listen in order to lead.

- Skill reduces the need for luck.

- Obsolescence is functional brokenness.

- Badness validates goodness. Goodness invalidates badness.

- Perfect intentions are the mother of imperfect results.

- All forms of evil are evil and often that evil is in human form.

- Do not let fear make you poor.

- You are what you make yourself out to be—nothing more and nothing less.

- Don't write more than what people want to read.

- You can't believe in the unthinkable if you don't believe in the thinkable.

- I took a page out of your one-page playbook.

- I am invigorated by the absence of your negativity.

- Tasks are completed only at the behest of the tasked.

- Usually, forward progress happens to those who think, solve, and execute.

- Those who do not learn from experience do not have experience worth learning.

- Show me a person who has only imagined, and I will show you a dreamer who is not accomplished.

- Revisionist creative thinking is the mother of innovation and change.

- Some things work better when you don't use them.

- Some people work better when you leave them alone.

- In some cases, a mediocre performance may be perfect enough for a good outcome.

- A perfect outcome may just need a mediocre performance.

- The flawed premise of equality should not be the basis of any country's foundation.

- Ignoring a problem only feeds it.

- Ignoring a problem is a bigger problem than the problem itself.

- Morality is measured more by sincere acts of compassion than by humans' mere scrolled platitudes on sacred sheets of paper.

- Turning a blind eye waters the root of all problems.

- Mindful acts come from heartfelt thoughts.

- Those of few words may have words with many meanings.

- It merits no wisdom to be smart in the dumber things in life.

- Wisdom is the artful mix of both fact and fiction.

- Wisdom should be shared and never have to be reinvented.

- Novices become experts by prudent practice in their craft.

- In reality, one should only be bribed with the priceless currency of honesty.

- One must sacrifice for the good of someone else.

- You will not create your Picasso with the first stroke of the brush. It takes commitment and time to create any masterpiece.

- One man's ignorance is another man's job security.

- Enemies are often befriended as a result of lies masked as truths.

- Wrongdoing is the summation of connivance and ignorance.

- No good mission can be achieved by soaking oneself in the sorrows of sadness or the joys of happiness.

- My description of your bad actions should not be your defining moment.

- Give a sloth a crutch and it will always hobble.

- Leaders must give equal fanfare in times of glory and gloom.

- Only believe a liar whose lips are sealed.

- Compromising to the liking of only one party is no compromise at all.

- Only true righteousness abounds in the souls of both the abolitionist and the enslaved.

- The ceiling of prosperity must be attainable by those in the basement of the economic ladder.

- All made up truths are lies.

- An apology should suture the wounds lashed by the tongue.

- Solving the matrices of man's mind and soul are the keys to understanding our human existence.

- Inspiration, dedication, and persistence are a wordsmith's trilogy of creativity.

- Reversing ignorance is never a backward task.

10.   Ignorance and Learning

- Dealing with ignorance is like pushing Jell-O through steel.

- Humans' indoctrination with ignorance leaves them blind with malicious intent.

- Connivance is purposeful lying about ignorance.

- The wise always makes sense from nonsense; the ignorant has it otherwise.

- Ignorance, ineptitude, and insubordination are poor defenses in any argument.

- To the simpleton, soft rumors are more believable than hard truths.

- The logic of your reasoning is as erroneous as the randomness of your conclusion.

- It may be all the same to be smart in dumb stuff as it is to be dumb in smart stuff.

- Look no further than to yourself as a teacher.

- Accidents are just unplanned, chaotic, life-learning events.

- Sometimes in life one should make mistakes well worth the error.

- Disagreements should not foster discordance but diversity of thought.

- When it comes to just about anything, the incorrectly educated may do more harm than the uneducated.

- One should not be educated by the ignorant but merely "learn" from them.

- College was merely the catalyst for a real education.

- Lessons learned in the past should be at the forefront of our learning for the present and the future.

- There is no acme in lifelong learning. Our minds should be "worn and wise" from usage, and not preserved in ignorance.

11.   Justice

- Listening to your silence on injustice is deafening.

- The justice I seek is the justice you deserve.

- I will not be denied the justice you will be served.

- Fostering social harmony, expanding inclusivity, and promoting justice amongst people and nations will entail making the economic floor of prosperity higher and firmer.

- Sometimes, a person must serve the country that often does not serve them.

- I will always serve the country that serves me.

- The revealed hidden histories of human bondage will now balance the scales of justice.

12.   Life and Death

- The value of a life is more than the sum of its events.

- Life can be a crapshoot that you better not be crappy at.

- Life is always having a problem to solve.

- Live a little! Only dead people should be dead.

- Life is not always meant to be conveniently comfortable.

- Life should always have some degree of meaningful discomfort.

- If you are not living on the edge, you might have fallen over it.

- Living life is a lifetime risk.

- Life can be planned. Birth and death, not so much.

- Birth, life, and death are the trilogy of our existence, but only life offers us direction, purpose, and character.

- Since death is for eternity, I want to live long to make it somewhat less than eternal.

- Death foreshortened is life prolonged.

- Death requires no preparation.

- No one dies too early or too late; everyone dies right on time—when they are supposed to.

- Unlike life, death can be comfortable.

- Unlike death, life is always eventful.

- There is no climate change in death. It's either hot, cold or indifferent.

- I know when I am going to die because it just so happens it will be at the end of my life.

- In death, there are no appointments—just walk-ins.

- You can't change appointments with death.

- While living, you can escape death all you want; but in the end, nobody is an escape artist.

- In cards, life may hold all the kings and queens, but death always holds the aces.

- I plan on dying on my own watch because only I will have a clear view.

- Die old because, in death, youth is not preserved.

- "Stay woke" while living because you can't once you're dead.

- Birth is the best decision I never made.

- There is no use maintaining an empty mind or an unused body for death.

- In death, one has no more memories to make, only those to keep.

- With its many branches, the tree of life has but one root.

- Life is a time continuum that should start with joy, may end in sorrow, and in between, is filled with healthy doses of both.

- There are only natural deaths in our natural world.

- An unnatural death is as common as an unnatural universe.

- There is nothing unnatural about the universe, and that includes life and death.

- Life is the beginning of eternity of which there is no end.

- Life comes with changes, challenges, and consequences.

- Any mix of chaos and monotony ensures a life of uncertain expectations.

- All of life's journeys lead to a dead end. Make sure your journey is one to die for.

- Living is a skilled event that, with mastery, will not need much luck or prayer to complete without a hitch.

- Suicide pays a disservice to the village that raised you.

- What I have lost to you in life, death may give vengeance a chance.

- To my enemies, in death my legacy will take vengeance on you.

- If life and death were like the weather they would not always be gloomy.

- We are created imperfectly and then life may make us even more so.

- Life is the only race worth running with death as its just reward.

- Death can be predicted but usually not in manner, method, or meaning.

- You must be in constant battle with your life's goals to stay current.

- The path to death, though well-travelled, is never worn.

13.   Medicine, Health, and Science

- Some diseases are not discovered; they are habitually invented.

- Only the lucky and the dead don't take medicine.

- I used to think that only cats and dogs took their medication reluctantly, and then I became a doctor.

- Good medication is just like good advice: take it and swallow it with your pride.

- The most important medical test is the one you need but don't have!

- "No salt" should be the only salt substitute.

- Obesity would render us unrecognizable to our ancestors.

- Most of us have been at our ideal body weight. It's just that some of us have passed it on the way up.

- Beware of genetic testing, for it may tell you who you really are and shatter who you really thought you were.

- The DNA that created us in the past will reinvent us in the future.

- Considering all the human maladies of mind, body, and soul, a healthy birth by good fortune or dumb luck is all the same to me.

- "Geo-psychosocial delusion" is never knowing where, whom, or what you are.

- As a doctor, I am only important to whom I serve.

- Phantom pain is not fake pain.

- A physician's patient-care mission is twofold: treat disease and eliminate fear.

- Being a doctor requires acceptance of the limitations of your patients, your knowledge, and yourself.

- Good Samaritan physicians will reveal a malady they were not searching for.

- Efficient, effective, and essential execution of duties makes a doctor a true healer.

- God made humans better than doctors can remake them.

- Our medical profession is not important because of us. We are important because of it.

- Medical care for the poor and the underserved is no more than a hologram in some instances—ghostlike in substance, structure, and service.

- Health care is a community of many services.

- Health care must begin first at the doorsteps of our patients.

- In any health care environment, it is unwise to invest solely in single-service structures.

- Save more souls than the soul you have.

- Patients are some of the greatest sources of knowledge, experience, and spirituality.

- Medical hysteria has gotten to the point where patients fear the unlikely more than the likely.

- In medicine, there usually is but only a small window of opportunity to do what is right for the ill patient.

- In humanity, nature provides the foreground, and nurture the background.

- Sometimes phenotype hides our genotypic commonality.

- Epigenetics and nature are what make identical twins not identical.

- Scientifically, climate—not humans—should be the only thing that gives privilege to skin color.

- Melanin is evolutionarily and genetically engineered solar protection.

- Melanin is the skin-deep, evolutionary, solar chemical armor.

- Our biogenetics link us more than the "geo-racial politics" that divide us.

- Science and ingenuity know no religion, race, or creed—only creativity and imagining the impossible.

- In dying of Alzheimer's disease, a once vibrant soul gave a long, valiant goodbye.

- Humanity must not allow the electronic age of medicine to erase the verbal communication age of medicine.

- The Vaccine Parental Paradox (TVPP) is the parental fear of disease prevention more than the disease itself.

- Illness, injury, and injustice have created unnecessary and costly disparities among us.

- The Vaccine Parental Paradox (TVPP) is the parental fear of ensuring disease prevention more than the disease itself.

- Patient disease hysteria is fearing the unlikely more than the likely.

14.   Memory

- Learning, forgetting, and relearning keep our memory in a constant state of flux and preservation.

- Unforgettable is eternal remembrance.

15. Men and Women

- The womb and the bosom are the origin and the sustenance of humankind.

- I would not mind if women ran the world, provided they don't take their cues from the men who do.

16.   Parents and Children

- Your children are a measure of who you are.

- Our children are our joint genetic material to the end of time.

- As children, we each have had different experiences with our parents, simply because we are different.

- Children are different. They must be treated fairly but not necessarily equally.

- Fair treatment is not the same as equal treatment.

- Some children demand everything, for which they do nothing.

- Children are the future of the history they will make.

- First, they are your parents, then your friends, and, lastly, your children.

- Each of us has an original mother to whom we owe our existence.

17.   Past, Present, and Future

- Going blindly into the future mires you in the past.

- In order to see into the future, you must live in the present and have witnessed the past.

- Our past will always be long, our future will always disappear, and our present will only be a moment at best.

- The present will judge man's misdeeds of the past.

- Investing in our youth is exchanging the past with the future through the power of the present.

- Your youth is the model for your future self.

- Although gone, all of the past is in the rearview mirror for us to draw from.

- If my past has not discouraged me, then the future should not.

- There is no future, and there is no past; there is only the present.

- The past and the future are nonexistent and unattainable. It is only the infinitesimal present that exists and is worth living.

- It is unwise to put the past behind you.

- An infinite number of probable and improbable futures are distilled by one present into a singular, definitive past.

- The present converts the fiction of many futures into the facts of one past.

- Asynchrony of time- one man's past should not be another man's future.

- Pay heed to the history of our past, the joy of our present, and the mystery of our future.

- The summation of the past and a distinct approaching future have led us to a singular present.

- The present is the catalyst that converts infinite futures into one indelible and unattainable past.

- There are infinite futures that are distilled into one distinct and singular past.

18.   **Perception and Self-Awareness**

- Do not be the last to love thyself.

- The one person you should see eye to eye with is yourself.

- Only a strong person can see the weakness within.

- Today is always an opportunity to be better than yesterday.

- Our vision must not be blinded by our sight.

- Optimists, pessimists, and realists each see a different side of the same thing.

19.   Politics and Political Correctness

- Being politically incorrect is like eating soup with a fork.

- Being politically incorrect is not believing in climate change as it burns you.

- An infant has an excuse for being politically incorrect: it's called ignorance.

- Political incorrectness is doing something that you shouldn't. Political correctness is doing something that you should, even though you may not want to.

- Politicians give lip service when they have no favors to get.

- The politics of our time are steeped more in currency than in courage.

- The irony of capitalism is that it cannot afford the luxuries of socialism.

- The definitional purpose of our G-PERMS humanitarian paradigms must not be framed by the partisan nature of our pundits, politicians, and puppets. (G-PERMS: Geo-Political, Economic, Religious, Moral, and Social paradigms)

- Pundits, politicians, and puppeteers purposefully serve only themselves.

- Understanding peoples, places, and politics is understanding culture.

20. Racism, Bigotry, and Humankind

- The racist seed was planted long ago. Now, we have its tree with its many branches of injustice, indifference, and inequality.

- Racially motivated economic injustice is economic injustice for all.

- Bigotry comes in all colors and so does humanity.

- Racists do not acknowledge their racism, because they are racist. Just like liars do not acknowledge their lies, because they are liars.

- Ironically, the profits and promotion of slavery outweighed the value of the life, liberty, and land of the South.

- The doctrines of racism and bigotry can make a people go against their own self-interests.

- The color differential, not commonness of country, has defined our alliances.

- Once our society understands that it has fundamental racial inequalities, then and only then will all lives truly matter.

- Being xenophobic is like having an allergy to humankind.

- Suffering the slights and savagery of slavery hardened the resistance of the oppressed.

- Racism is never equally bidirectional.

- Racism and bigotry are mechanistic tools used to chisel artificial differences between peoples to deny opportunities, withhold access, and limit resources to some while providing the same to others.

- The evil triplets of racism, sexism, and bigotry are nurtured on the bosoms of ignorance and privilege.

21.   Rights, Privileges, and Responsibilities

- In a truly free and fair society, there should be no privileges, only rights.

- Remember, it is the Bill of Rights, *not* the Bill of Privileges.

- Privilege is only what the past has allowed and what the future will allow you to have.

- Your *convenience* should not be at my *inconvenience*.

- Poverty and privilege rarely come as a pair.

- Ultimate privilege is having access to everything and consequences for nothing.

- Wealth and opportunity have been reserved for the privileged few.

- Without much responsibility, one can be as self-assured as one wants.

- Wealth and privilege are expensed on the masses.

- Pockets of poverty must be filled in by the wealth of our society.

- We have a moral obligation to eliminate the pockets and pitfalls of poverty.

22.   Slavery and Oppression

- Resistance and rebellion, courage and compassion severed the chains of human bondage.

- The creative spark was dimmed but not extinguished by the injustice of human bondage.

- Slavery and genocide must be part of the dialogue about our country's founding as they were in reality.

- Neither the slow friction of time nor indentured servitude extinguished the resolve of the forgotten and the forsaken.

- Sadly, slavery and indentured servitude of the poor are foundational to the privilege and prosperity of the rich.

- John Brown demonstrated racial reconciliation in his willingness to sacrifice his privilege and life for the lives of the enslaved.

- John Brown's high bar of abolition was achieved by no other puritan, politician, or pundit of his time nor mine.

- Unbeknownst to the master, the slave was often the benefactor of his own ingenuity.

- Deceit and greed often are the engines that oppress.

- The oppressed were never the intended benefactors of any dream.

- The human condition of the oppressed has always been adversely affected by the deceit of the oppressor.

- Profiting off the labors of the oppressed is the true measure of laziness.

- It is resistance, not laziness, when one does not toil for the prosperity of others.

- Poverty is the cruelest disparity.

- Oppression is one way to ruin humanity.

- No statues, no words, and no decrees will absolve those who enslaved their fellow humans.

- Slavery and its wicked cousin, racism, make a mockery of our doctrines and declarations.

- The Middle Passage, the triangle of death, destitution, and despair, could not conquer the grit of the African diaspora.

- The trauma of the Middle Passage has been etched in the souls' of our DNA.

- The Middle Passage traverses the largest watery human burial ground of a stolen people.

- The souls of slaves haunt the Atlantic's watery graves.

- Those who stood proudly with honor to uphold the injustices of slavery and human bondage will always stand and be remembered as being on the wrong side of humanity.

- Behold, in death, God will not deny justice for the enslaved as She serves justice to the enslavers.

- Our freedom has been eroded by the slow friction of time.

- Slavery and human bondage were "wealth-force-multipliers" for the few, the favored, and the feckless.

- Slavery soldered each link in the chain of economic prosperity.

- Each link in the chain of economic prosperity was powered by slavery.

- The oppressed have been shackled by the narrative of the majority opinion.

- There must be no dementia or programmed amnesia when it comes to the significance of slavery in our world.

- The postbellum narrative was designed to mentally enslave the now made free.

- Only the slave and the abolitionist do not sanitize historical truths.

23.   Success and Failure

- In a virtuous world, one should only fail at being perfect.

- Failed attempts of perfection should be one's only failure in life.

- There is no measure of success in being 99% right only 1% of the time.

- Success offers only a small margin for learning.

- Achieving one's goals requires a certain amount of success and failure but slightly more of the former and slightly less of the latter.

- Achieve or don't achieve, succeed or don't succeed, you are who you are.

- Developing your skill reduces your need to rely on pure luck for success.

- One carries more weight with lighter words.

- Whims and wishes are not the makeup of a leader worth following.

- In reality we are defeated by our lack of communication skills and absence of redundancy of purpose.

- Failure is a perfect opportunity to learn how not to fail.

- As long as we can adapt, failure is our best mentor.

- Procrastination is a benign form of sabotage.

- Failure increases one's margin for learning.

- Learning is maximized by the degree and number of successful and unsuccessful risks taken.

24.   Time

- Time is always a good predictor of what will happen.

- Time measures all things fairly and equally.

- Humanity is painted on the easel of time.

- Your beauty has transcended the machinations of time.

- There is no future in following a clock that has run out of time.

- All deeds are timeless measures of our character.

- The slow *friction of time* has effortlessly etched our vices and virtues in the verses of history.

- Procrastination exacerbates the friction of time.

- Creativity of mind is often spurred by limitations in, and friction of, time.

- Programmed procrastination is a well-planned waste of time.

- Opportunists are spatially and temporally in the right place at the right time.

- God judges humans equally and timelessly.

- Being an enemy of time is truly a waste of time.

- The time one shares with others should be priceless.

- Be most expeditious when time is lacking.

- Only those with no ambition should worry most about the passage of time.

- Time affords procrastination and productivity equal measure.

- The best prophet is time.

25.   Violence and War

- Violence and the weapons of violence have stolen the inner fabric of our youth.

- Wars are fueled with the flesh of the less than fortunate and the forgotten.

- Camouflaging deceit is an art of war.

- In war and in peace, a taxed coin far outweighs a taxed cow.

- A warrior's greatest weapon against war is his or her compassion for the vanquished.

- Every soldier must learn the lessons of warfare history to understand the mission.

- War is better understood through the opaque mettle of passions, principles, and politics than through the polished metal of bullets, bombs, and bayonets.

- Battlefield dynamics should be approached as a time, space, element continuum.

- I lay my arms down, for there are no more battles for me to fight.

- The atrocities of war should be told from the mouths of the ones who have lost the most and gained the least.

- War is colorblind to the blood it sheds.

- There is no alternate template of humans in war, for they are "makers of misery."

- Some humans have an innate desire for conquest by malice.

- Although the future is uncertain, it may hold a period when wars are entirely cyberspace-based and winners and losers are defined by "bits and bytes" instead of by "blood and bones."

- There is no alternate template of man in war — either he is the offender or the defender of humankind's interests.

- Winning wars is more a matter of systems of technique than systems of technology.

- Against reasonable foes, if armed with aphorisms one does not need a sword to do battle.

- Wars are won more by creative minds than by the machines those minds created.

- War, man's malevolent aggression in perpetuity, is the product of ignorance of differing Geo-Political, Economic, Religious, Moral, and Social (G-PERMS) constructs.

- It is a human choice— peace or war!

- There is no better person to compliment you than your greatest enemy.

- Deceptive tactics blind an enemy to what they should see from what they want to see.

- Sometimes even the victor cannot bring order to battlefield chaos.

26. Miscellaneous

Preparation

- The best way to get rid of doubt is to prepare, practice, and perform.

- Preparation creates the absence of doubt.

- A pinprick of preparation may pierce a balloon full of doubt.

Religion

- Religion, race, and rank are humans' trifecta for war and barriers to peace.

- Religion, race, and rank have been the roots of war, slavery, and genocide.

- Religion has made evil souls of the greedy.

- Greedy souls have weaponized religion for worldly exploits.

- Humankind's religious misdeeds have created the evil we worship.

- Wars of enslavement have been weaponized by humans' perversion of religion.

Talking, Tweeting, and Texting

- More talking, tweeting, and texting often converts common sense into nonsense.

- One flaw of talking too much is adding nonsense to the sense you make.

- Fact and fiction make for a story worth telling.

- One does not need to yell to have a voice.

Words

- Wise words from the voices of the known or unknown should never fall on deaf ears.

- Simple words with pithy meanings are better than pithy words with simple meanings.

- Some people know the right thing to say but may be the wrong ones to say it.

- Sometimes the wrong people may say the right thing.

- The mouth of a "rum-filled mind" spills lies and truths with equal weight.

- Sadly, my words of wisdom may fall on deaf ears, for I am neither famous nor infamous.

Wrong

- At least you know where you stand if you are consistently wrong versus inconsistently right.

- There may be more honor in being consistently wrong than inconsistently right.

- Not many are 100 percent right 1 percent of the time.

Singletons

- Adversity is handled best by a steady hand, a kind soul, and a warm heart.

- You can't play the game both ways.

- An example should be made of the poor one you are.

- I want to wring the wrong out of your words, actions, and thoughts.

- If I had more money, I would give bigger tips.

- Well-fed fish do not bite for the worm.

- Involvement means listening, learning, and living.

- Only the awakened should sleep for enjoyment.

- Longevity of service fosters cohesion; brevity of service fosters discord.

- An unchecked need for greed permeates the world of politics and economics alike.

- Poor people save more food than they waste; rich people waste more food than they save.

- A secret is only a secret if only you know it.

- God will not keep your secrets.

- There are no secrets in the world that are known by only one person.

- Always be on the right side of a two-sided story.

- There is no need for shelter; the shade you throw is shelter enough.

- We will not be discouraged, we will not be deterred, and we will not be defeated by our enemies.

- The wicked are misled by their imagination.

About the Author

Dr. Dante Pierre Galiber is a cardiologist who practices on St. Croix, US Virgin Islands, and is Director of Cardiology at the Governor Juan F. Luis Hospital. He is married to Yvonne Ashley and they have a daughter, Dominique Ashley, a 2019 graduate of Temple University. A native Crucian, Dr. Galiber was born on November 26, 1963. He was the 1982 valedictorian at St. Dunstan's Episcopal High School on St. Croix, an early admissions student, a Barnett Frank Award recipient at the University of the Virgin Islands, National Merit Scholarship Finalist, and a *magna cum laude* Howard University graduate. He is a member of *Phi Beta Kappa* Honor Society and an honorary member of Golden Key International Honour Society. Galiber completed medical school and internal medicine training at Indiana University and an invasive cardiology fellowship at the University of Kansas. He is board certified in internal medicine, cardiology, and nuclear cardiology. He is a Major in the Virgin Islands Army National Guard and an avid tennis player.

About the Book

QFTQ, a writing odyssey, began in 2008 with medical essays punctuated with "spot-on sayings," and it continued as an ongoing project of documenting original quotations while working, playing tennis, or talking with friends and family. Moments of inspiration often prompted a pause in mid-conversation to record ideas or quotes that came to mind before they were lost to the cosmos forever. Diligence and "pen and paper" ensured that many great and meaningful quotes were recorded. Writing is an exhaustive exercise that captures sometimes transient thoughts for the world to see, read, and interpret for the good of humanity. Time, space, and human interaction provided the moment, the setting, and the inspiration for more than 450 quotations.